Working Dogs

Television and Movie Star Dogs

by Kimberly M. Hutmacher

Consulting Editor: Gail Saunders-Smith, PhD

Consultant: Jone Bouman,
American Humane Film and TV Unit

CAPSTONE PRESS
a capstone imprint

Pebble Plus is published by Capstone Press,
151 Good Counsel Drive, P.O. Box 669, Mankato, Minnesota 56002.
www.capstonepub.com

032010
005740CGF10

Books published by Capstone Press are manufactured with paper
containing at least 10 percent post-consumer waste.

Library of Congress Cataloging-in-Publication Data
Hutmacher, Kimberly.
  Television and movie star dogs / by Kimberly M. Hutmacher.
     p. cm.—(Pebble plus. Working dogs)
  Includes bibliographical references and index.
  Summary: "Simple text and full-color photos illustrate the traits, training, and duties of television and movie star
dogs"—Provided by publisher
  ISBN 978-1-4296-4471-6 (library binding)
  1. Dogs in motion pictures—Juvenile literature. 2. Dogs on television—Juvenile literature. 3. Show dogs—Juvenile
literature. 4. Motion picture actors and actresses—Juvenile literature. 5. Dogs—Training—Juvenile literature. I. Title.
II. Series.
  PN1995.9.A5H88 2011
  791.4302'80929—dc22   2009051417

Editorial Credits
Erika Shores, editor; Bobbie Nuytten, designer; Marcie Spence, media researcher; Eric Manske, production specialist

Photo Credits
Capstone Studio/Karon Dubke, cover (collar), 19
FOX 2000 PICTURES / THE KOBAL COLLECTION, 11
Getty Images Inc./CBS Photo Archive, 9; Michael Grecco/UpperCut Images, cover; Scott Barbour, 21
Globe Photos, 1, 15
Marisa Bellis, American Humane Association, on the set of Disney's Underdog, 17
Newscom, 7; 20th Century Fox/Tenner, Suzanne, 5
WALT DISNEY / THE KOBAL COLLECTION / LEDERER, JOSEPH, 13

**Capstone Press thanks the American Humane Film & TV Unit (www.americanhumane.org)
for their assistance in reviewing this book.**

Note to Parents and Teachers

The Working Dogs series supports national social studies standards related to people, places,
and culture. This book describes and illustrates television and movie star dogs. The images
support early readers in understanding the text. The repetition of words and phrases helps early
readers learn new words. This book also introduces early readers to subject-specific vocabulary
words, which are defined in the Glossary section. Early readers may need assistance to read
some words and to use the Table of Contents, Glossary, Read More, Internet Sites, and Index
sections of the book.

Table of Contents

Furry Stars

Some famous actors
have four legs and a tail.
Dogs star in movies and on TV.

Rin Tin Tin was the first famous movie dog. This German shepherd starred in 26 movies in the late 1920s.

A dog named Lassie was
a TV star in the 1950s.
Fans loved this friendly collie.

What It Takes to Be a Star

Acting dogs are all sizes and breeds. Often, more than one dog plays the same role. In *Marley & Me*, 22 Labrador retrievers played Marley.

11

TV and movie dogs need
to be calm. They work
in strange places.
They are around moving
cameras and bright lights.

Acting dogs are friendly
and smart. They get along
with new people and animals.
Acting dogs learn
commands quickly.

Training

Trainers work with acting dogs.
Before dogs can work,
trainers teach them to sit,
stay, and lie down.

Trainers can't be filmed.
They use hand signals
to tell a dog what to do.
Lowering a hand to the floor
tells a dog to lie down.

TV and movie dogs are

hardworking dogs.

When filming begins,

these furry stars are ready

to shine.

Glossary

breed—a group of animals that come from common relatives

command—an order to follow a direction

famous—known by many people

role—a part played by an actor in a movie or TV show

trainer—a person who teaches and guides other people or animals

Read More

Goldish, Meish. *Hollywood Dogs.* Dog Heroes. New York: Bearport, 2007.

Presnall, Judith Janda. *Animal Actors.* Animals with Jobs. San Diego: Kidhaven Press, 2002.

Internet Sites

FactHound offers a safe, fun way to find Internet sites related to this book. All of the sites on FactHound have been researched by our staff.

Here's all you do:

Visit *www.facthound.com*

FactHound will fetch the best sites for you!

Index

Word Count: 179
Grade: 1
Early-Intervention Level: 16